EMOTIONAL INTELLIGENCE

IMPORTANT IN DETERMINING PROFESSIONAL SUCCESS

DR. SAVITA MISHRA

Copyright © Dr. Savita Mishra
All Rights Reserved.

This book has been published with all efforts taken to make the material error-free after the consent of the author. However, the author and the publisher do not assume and hereby disclaim any liability to any party for any loss, damage, or disruption caused by errors or omissions, whether such errors or omissions result from negligence, accident, or any other cause.

While every effort has been made to avoid any mistake or omission, this publication is being sold on the condition and understanding that neither the author nor the publishers or printers would be liable in any manner to any person by reason of any mistake or omission in this publication or for any action taken or omitted to be taken or advice rendered or accepted on the basis of this work. For any defect in printing or binding the publishers will be liable only to replace the defective copy by another copy of this work then available.

Contents

Preface

Emotional Intelligence determines one's potential for learning the practical skills that are based on its five elements, self-awareness, motivation, self-regulation, empathy and adeptness in relationship. Emotional competence shows how much of the potential he has translated into on-the job capabilities. For instance, the ability to recognize accurately what other person is feeling enables one to develop a specific competency such as influence. Similarly, people who are able to regulate their emotions will find it easier to develop a competency such as Initiative or Achievement drive. Ultimately it is this Social and Emotional Competencies that we need to identify and measure if we want to be able to predict performances.

Emotional Intelligence involves the ability to perceive accurately, appraise and express emotion, the ability to access and/or generate feeling, when they facilitate the ability to understand emotion and emotional knowledge and the ability to regulate emotions to promote emotional and intellectual growth. Emotional intelligence is the accumulation of all cognitive, non-cognitive and non- physical capabilities, competencies and skills a person has that helps him/her to deal with the demand and pressure of everyday life. It is necessary for the leaders, supervisors, managers, colleagues and others in the workplace, to understand their emotions and their workers to get the quality productivity. In particular parents, teachers, supervisors, administrators, head of the institutions and others in the teaching-learning situation to know and understand their emotions and also their children for getting outstanding result in their respective areas.

Dr. Savita Mishra

CHAPTER ONE

EMOTIONAL INTELLIGENCE

Kothari commission (1964) reported that yesterday's education system cannot satisfy the present need and even less so, tomorrow's need. To meet the present need, the education of the youth should be changed from the world of school to the world of work and life. Perhaps today's education system hardly gives any guarantee for a successful life. Education in the contemporary society is not mere acquisition of Bookish knowledge, but in fact interaction between the teacher and the pupil, knowledge, understanding and handling the emotions in the right manner, at the right time, in the right way.

In the past, the main point of norms has been both for the school and the parents- the exclusive intellectual achievement in terms of higher percentage of marks in the Examination. While intellectual Excellence is highly desirable, exclusive emphasis on it, at the cost of other important aspect, is self – defeating (because in the long run, intellectual excellence requires emotional maturity) as well as functional, as it produces anxiety and depression in children. There is a need to bring about a balance by giving due importance to the "non-intellectual" or emotional aspects of one's growth. Our past experience and experiments clearly delineate that even a person with a high intellect cannot be always successful. But why is it so? This vacuum is realized over the years. Many psychologists and educationist have been trying to bridge a gap between the success and discomfiture caused by head (value) and heart (devalue). The logical inquiry continues over the years not only in developing countries like India but all over the world.

HISTORICAL ROOTS

When psychologists began to write and think about intelligence they focused on cognitive aspects, such as memory and problem-solving. However, there was research that recognized early on the non-cognitive aspects were also important. For instance, avid Wechsler defined intelligence as the "the aggregate or global capacity of the individual to act purposefully, to think rationally, and to deal effectively with his environment." As early as 1940 he referred to "Non-Intellective" as well as "Intellective elements", by which he meant affective, personal, and social factors. Furthermore, as early as 1943 Wechsler was proposing that the non-intellective abilities are essential for predicting one's ability to succeed in life.

EMOTIONAL INTELLIGENCE: CONCEPTUAL ANALYSIS

Psychologist Mayer, et al. (1989) coined the term Emotional Intelligence, though it was referred by various names - from smartness and personality to soft skills and competence. Emotional Intelligence contains two major aspects "Emotions" and "Intelligence". Emotion is as any agitation or disturbance of mind, passion, any achievement or excited mental state. Emotions or feelings have both a psychological component and cognitive element that influence behavior. Intelligence is the capacity to understand the word, think rationally and use resources effectively when faced with challenges. Emotional Intelligence refers to the ability required for efficient living.

The term emotional intelligence has been rooted from the social intelligence, which was first coined by EL Thorndike in 1920. In 1985, Reuven Bar-on invented the term Emotional Quotient (E.Q i.e. E.Q is a relative measure of one's emotional intelligence possessed by Lim at a particular period of his life) to describe his approach to evaluating general intelligence. In the first time Peter Salovey of Yale and John Mayer of University of NE Hamishire (1990) conceptualized the term Emotional Intelligence that consisted of three different categories of adaptive abilities. Firstly, it is appraisal and expression in the self as well as others. In the self there are verbal and non-verbal components, in the others there are non-verbal perception and empathy. Secondly there is regulation of emotion in the self and others. Thirdly, it is utilization of emotion that includes flexible planning, redirected attention and motivation. Daniel Goleman (1995) and American psychologist then subsumed this definition with a lot of personality characteristics, which he believed would contribute positively to success in any domain of life. Goleman (1999) Emotional Intelligence encompasses the following five characteristics and abilities.

Personal Competence: These competencies determine how we manage ourselves.

Self-awareness: Knowing what we are feeling in the moment and using those preferences to guide our decision making, having a realistic assessment of our own abilities and a well-grounded sense of self-confidence. Emotional awareness-Recognizing one's emotions and their effect. Accurate Self assessment- Knowing one's strengths and limits. Self-confidence: A strong sense of one's self-worth and capabilities.

Self Regulation (moods managements): Managing one's internal states, impulses and resources. Self control: Keeping disruptive emotions and Band integrity. Conscientiousness: taking responsibility for personal performance. Adaptability: Flexibility in handling change. Innovation: Being comfortable with novel ideas, approaches and new information.

Self-Motivation: Emotional tendencies that guide or facilitate reaching goals. Achievements drive: Aligning with the goals of the groups or organization. Initiative: Readiness to act on opportunities. Optimism: Persistence in pursuing goals despite obstacles and setbacks.

Social Competence: These competencies determine how we handle relationships.

Empathy: Awareness of others feeling needs and concerns. Understanding others: Sensing others feeling and perspective, and taking an active interest in their concerns. Developing others: Sensing others development needs and bolstering their abilities. Service Orientation: Anticipating, recognizing and meeting customer's needs. Leveraging diversity: Cultivating opportunities through different kinds of people. Political awareness: Reading a group emotional currents and power relationships.

Social Skills: (Managing relationships): Adeptness at inducing desirable response in others. Influence: Wielding effective tactics for persuasion. Communication: Listening openly and sending convincing messages. Conflict Managements: Negotiating and resolving disagreements. Leadership: Inspiring and guiding individuals and groups. Change catalyst: Initiating or managing change. Building bounds: Nurturing instrumental relationship. Collaboration and co-operation: Working with others toward shared goals. Team capabilities: Creating group synergy in pursuing collective goals.

1.1.2. EMOTIONAL COMPETENCE AND EMOTIONAL INTELLIGENCE

Goleman has made a distinction between Emotional Intelligence and Emotional Competence. Emotional Competence refers to the personal and social skills that lead to superior performance in the world of work so an Emotional Competence is a learned capability based on emotional intelligence that result in outstanding performance at work. A certain level of emotional intelligence is necessary to learn the emotional competencies. Take the fineness shown by the flight attendant. She was superb at influence, and important emotional competence getting others to respond in a desired way. At the heart of this competence are two abilities empathy, which involves reading the feelings of others, and social skills, which handling those feelings artfully.

Whereas Emotional Intelligence determines one's potential for learning the practical skills that are based on its five elements, self-awareness, motivation, self-regulation, empathy and adeptness in relationship. Emotional competence shows how much of the potential he has translated into on- the job capabilities. For instance, the ability to recognize accurately what other person is feeling enables one to develop a specific competency such as influence. Similarly, people who are able to regulate their emotions will find it easier to develop a competency such as Initiative or Achievement drive. Ultimately it is this social and Emotional Competencies that we need to identify and measure if we want to be able to predict performances.

Mayer and Salovey (1997) revised their own definitions stressing the cognitive components of Emotional Intelligence and described "Emotional Intelligence involves the ability to perceive accurately, appraise and express emotion, the ability to access and/or generate feeling, when they facilitate the ability to understand emotion and emotional knowledge and the ability to regulate emotions to promote emotional and intellectual growth". This definition was referred to the mental abilities of the organism. A more formal academic definition refers to emotional awareness and emotional management skills, which provide the ability to balance emotion and reason so as to maximize long term happiness. In general we can define emotional intelligence as the accumulation of all cognitive, non-cognitive and non-physical capabilities, competencies and skills a person has that helps him/her to deal with the demand and pressure of everyday life.

1.1.3. Characteristics of Emotional Intelligence

- It is a non-cognitive and non-physical capacity of the organism.
- It is an internal or psychological process, which motivates the organism to perform its activities properly.
- It is nurturable.

- It energizes the organism to accomplish the required tasks.
- Level of emotional intelligence is neither genetically fixed nor does it develop only in early childhood and develop throughout life.

1.1.4. EMOTIONAL INTELLIGENCE (E.Q) AND GENERAL INTELLIGENCE (IQ)

General Intelligence is the aggregate or global capacity of an individual to act purposefully, to think rationally and deal effectively with his environment. Whereas Emotional Intelligence is the capacity or ability to understand one's own emotions, the emotions of other and appropriately based on these emotions. Intelligence refers to the cognitive abilities of the organism. However, emotional intelligence refers to the non-cognitive and no-physical capacities of the organism. So, emotional Intelligence is nurturable and general intelligence is inherited and not nurturable. Level of general intelligence is genetically fixed, whereas emotional intelligence is neither genetically fixed nor does it develop only in early childhood and develop throughout life.

Our past research evidences suggest that "Emotional Intelligence can be more powerful than intelligent quotient". When IQ defines how smart a person is? In the meantime E.I. defines how well person knows how smart he is? According to Goleman, IQ accounts for only about 20 percent of person's success in life. The remaining 80 percent depend largely on person's emotional intelligence i.e. E.Q.

Why emotional intelligence is significant for every sphere of life in general, and teaching-learning situation in particular? In general, it is necessary for the leaders, supervisors, managers, colleagues and others in the workplace, to understand their emotions and their workers to get the quality productivity. In particular parents, teachers, supervisors, administrators, head of the institutions and others in the teaching-learning situation to know and understand their emotions and also their children for getting outstanding result in their respective areas.

1.1.5. IMPORTANCE OF EMOTIONAL INTELLIGENCE

Research in brain-based learning suggests that emotional health is fundamental to effective learning. According to report from the National Center for clinical infant programmes, the most critical element for a student's success in school is an understanding of how to learn. The key ingredients for this understanding are: Confidence, curiosity, intentionality, self-control, relatedness, capacity to communicate and ability to cooperate.

These traits are all aspects of Emotional Intelligence. Emotional Intelligence has proven a better predictor of future success than traditional methods like the GPA (Grade Point Average, it is an American Terminology), IQ and standardized test score. Emotional Intelligence plays a pivotal role in designing the required personality; build up the emotional maturity suitable to the age, build up the ability in the self-adaptation for solving the stress problems and the pressure of life in the competing status of an individual.

The enhancement of the harmonious personality of the individual depends to a large extent on his/her emotional intelligence. It enables a man to achieve highest pinnacle and deepest reach in his search for self-fulfillment as well as others fulfillment. Attributing quantitative values to qualitative phenomena that is evident from the all pervasive marks system which rapidly becomes the dominant goal of pupils. Therefore, emotional intelligence is very important aspect on which depends the future career of the children.

Emotional Intelligence can enable teacher to resolve past issues and both external as well as internal conflicts, help them to attain emotional power and accomplish their goals at all levels physical, mental, spiritual and emotional and also improve psychological abilities such as memory, clarity of thinking and decision- making.

Emotional Intelligence is a primary factor in healthy ageing permitting the human being to live long as well and it is positively impact to the individual ability to sustain both mental and physical health. Emotional Intelligence also enables to assume responsibility for an individual's feeling by saying "I feel" instead of "I should not have".

Emotional Intelligence helps in stimulating motivation, improving communication, reducing stress and enhancing decision-making power of teachers, administrators, students and also parents. Emotional Intelligence also helps to cope with stressful situations stress managements, therefore large by depends upon striking an emotional balance between a potential stress condition and reaction to it.

Researchers Gill, 2003 and Ghosh 2003 have described that children with high EQ are more confident, are better learners, have higher self-esteem, have few behavioral problems, are more optimistic and happier, handle their emotion better and even to be a successful entrepreneur one needs to have a high emotional intelligence.

The study of Abraham (1999) revealed that EQ was theorized to have a positive effect on organizational outcomes of work group-cohesion, congruence between self and supervisor appraisals of performance, employee performance, organizational commitments and organizational citizenship. It may also prevent emotional dissonance ethical role conflict and job insecurity from effecting organizational commitments. The most beneficial effects of emotional intelligence may occur in environment in which there is a high degree of job control.

David Wachsher (1940), recognized through his research that, non-intellective abilities are essential for predicting one's ability to success in life. In 1990 Salovey and Mayer found emotional intelligence as a form of social intelligence that involves the ability to monitor one's own and other's feeling and emotions, to discriminate among them, and to use this information to guide one's thinking and action. Goleman (1990) in his research found the importance of social and emotional abilities for personal success. IQ by itself is not a very good predictor of job performance. Hunter and Hunter estimated that at least IQ accounts for about 25 percent of the variance. Sternberg has pointed out that studies vary and that 10 percent may be more realistic estimate. In some studies, IQ accounts for as little as 4 percent of the variance. About the limits of IQ as a predictor is the Summerville study, a 40 year longitudinal investigating of 450 boys who grew up in Summerville, Massachusetts where found, IQ had little relating to how well they did at work or in the rest of their lives. What made the biggest difference was childhood abilities such as being above to handle frustration, control, emotions and get along with other people. A study of 80 Ph. D.S in science who underwent a better of personality test, IQ test and interviews in the 1950s when they were in their early seventies, they were tracked down and estimates were made of their success based on resumed evaluations by experts in their own fields, and sources like American men and women of science. It turned out that social and emotional abilities were four times more important than IQ in determining professional success and prestige. There is research in the "Marsh mallow studies" at Standford University suggested that emotional and social skills actually help improve cognitive functioning.

Adolescents need to develop empathy, self-awareness, self-regulations, social skills and other competences of emotional intelligence in order to grow socially and emotionally for a better world of prosperity. Hence there has been a need in assessing the emotional intelligence of adolescents and provide necessary guidance to see the better world. A number of researchers have already been conducted in the western countries as well as in India considering the developmental psychology. From the conceptualization point of view it is evident that assessment of emotional intelligence and the factors that correlates to emotional intelligence need to be reviewed for arriving at the problem under study.

1.2. RATIONALE OF THE STUDY

Emotional Intelligence has not traditionally seen the amount of research or exploration that has been given to topics such as cognitive intelligence, mental health and mental capabilities. Since emotion plays a vital role in the ways human interact with each other and perform in home, school and work settings, the need to undertake emotion and Emotional Intelligence is obvious.

Emotional Intelligence is the driving force behind the factors that affect personal success and everyday interaction with others. Studies of Emotional Intelligence have shown its relevance on many aspects of life and the role it plays in the interaction and discussions of any given day. Emotional Intelligence predicts as much as 80% of a person's success in life, whereas IQ predicts about 20%.

According to Goleman (1995) Research indicates that there is a relationship between Emotional Intelligence and leadership. Because of research in these areas, recent publications and continued progressive thinking in regard to the topic, Emotional Intelligence and its implication have been brought to the attention of educators and researchers across the nation. However, as almost all Emotional Intelligence research target adults, a need exists for the exploration of adolescent's Emotional Intelligence.

Considering the importance of Emotional Intelligence in relation to adolescence phase from the reviews stated above, the present investigation has been proposed to be undertaken. Hence, the problem aims to explore the relationship of specific age and gender variables adolescents' emotional intelligence. Whether the demographic variables of age and gender have any impact in the emotional intelligence of secondary school is the main aim of the study.

1.3. OBJECTIVES

For this study, the following objectives have been framed:

- To assess the Emotional Intelligence of senior secondary school students with respect to their age and gender.
- To compare the levels of emotional intelligence of senior secondary school students in relation to intra & inter-personal awareness and intra

& inter-personal management.

- To categorize them under differential levels of emotional intelligence along the lines of normality in a five point scale.
- To find differential levels of emotional intelligence due to age and gender variations.

1.4. FORMULATION OF HYPOTHESIS

The following hypotheses have been formulated in null form keeping in view the objectives of the study:

Ho1: Emotional Intelligence in senior secondary school students is not normally displayed.

Ho2: There doesn't exist significant difference in intrapersonal awareness of senior secondary school students due to gender variation.

H03: There doesn't exist significant difference in interpersonal awareness of senior secondary school students due to gender variation.

Ho4: There doesn't exist significant difference in intrapersonal management of senior secondary school students due to gender variation.

Ho5: There doesn't exist significant difference in interpersonal management of senior secondary school students due to gender variation.

Ho6: There doesn't exist significant difference in Emotional Intelligence of senior secondary school students due to age variation.

H07: There doesn't exist significant difference in Emotional Intelligence of senior secondary school students due to gender variation.

1.5. OPERATIONAL DEFINITIONS

Assessment: Assessment will be done by administering the questionnaires.

Emotional Intelligence: In this study, emotional intelligence refer to inter and Intra - personal awareness and management as per Mangal and Mangal (2009).

Senior Secondary School Students: Students between the age group of 17-18 yrs. and reading in classes XI – XII in 5 different senior secondary schools.

1.6. SCOPE AND DELIMITATION

Due to stringency of time and money in collecting data only 100 students of classes XI and XII from Senior Secondary Schools were considered for the study. The scope of this study is limited to the extent of assessing Emotional Intelligence of students with respect to their gender and age. The study is delimited to students of classes XI and XII of 5 Senior Secondary

Schools only.

CHAPTER TWO

REVIEW OF RELATED LITERATURE

2.1. Review of Related Literature

Wechsler (1940) referred to "non-intellective" as well as "intellective" elements by which he meant affective, personal and social factors and in 1943 he found out that non-intellective abilities are essential for predicting one's ability to succeed in life.

Rotter (1954) found locus control, i.e. Individuals who have a low perception of such contingencies, are said to have an internal locus of control; whereas those who attribute a great importance to outside forces influencing outcomes are said to have an external locus of control.

Lefcourt (1976) found in the research on the relationship between internality and deferred gratification-persistence in working towards a goal and a willingness to defer gratification to immediate needs, one's undivided attention and the highest priority to the task in hand. Since internals believe that their efforts lead to favourable outcomes, they rely on their own understanding and predict ability. Externals, on the other hand, perceiving a lack of predictability and fearing the unforeseen external factors that could affect the outcomes, find it easier to seek immediate gratification rather than work to achieve distant goals.

Duccette et.al. (1984) found that the correlation between achievement, motivation and preference for moderate risk was significant and positive among internals, but almost zero among externals.

Hardely and Ban-on (1988) reported that the air force committee found that most successful recruiters scored significantly higher in the Emotional Intelligence competencies.

Mayer, et.al. (1989) introduced the concept of Emotional Intelligence, through it was referred by various names – from smartness and personality to soft skills and competence.

Salovey et.al. (1990) in their research develop valid measures of emotional intelligence and explore its significance. They found in one study that when a group of people saw an upsetting film, those who scored high in emotional clarity (which is the ability to identify and give a name to a mood that is being experienced or recovered more quickly. In another study, they found individuals who scored higher in the ability to perceive accurately, understand and appraise other's emotions were better able to respond flexible to changes in their social environments and build supportive social networks.

Seligman (1991) found optimism is an attitude that buffers people from falling into apathy hopelessness like hope, optimism means having a strong expectation that, in general, things will turn out alright in life-despite setbacks and frustrations. People who are optimistic perceive the cause of failure to be something that can be changed. Optimism has been found to be success in various pursuits like academic work, business, health, politics, sports and religion.

Goleman (1995) found a study conducted on 15 Harvard students with high 10 who were followed up into their middle age. The study revealed that men with higher test scores in colleges were not particularly successful in productivity and status in their field. Also found to be highly dissatisfied and did not fare well in other spheres.

Mcctelland et.al. (1995) found how little traditional tests of cognitive intelligence told us about what it takes to be successful in life.

Spencer (1997) found out the executives of high achievement companies scored high Emotional Intelligence scores than the average executives. It showed that there was a positive relationship between Emotional intelligence and Business Achievement.

Bar-on (1998) found that the air force committee found that most successful recruiters scored significantly higher in the Emotional Intelligence Competencies.

Bachman (2000) found out the most successful Collectors scored significantly higher in the Emotional Intelligence Competencies like self-actualization, independence and optimism.

Cover & Murphy (2000) conducted a study that examined the relationship between self-identity and academic persistence and achievement in a counter stereotypical domain. The study revealed that the higher the self-concept and self-schema, the more positive the self-descriptions, the better the academic achievement at 18. The study also showed that self-identity improvers through interaction and communication with other which would enhance achievement.

Charbonneau et.al. (2001) in their study tested the validity of two measures of emotional intelligence (EI) and they investigated the relation between EI and leadership in 191 adolescents attending a 3 weeks military training camp. A scale by Schutte et. al. assessed primarily the interpersonal aspect of EI, whereas selected items from the weisinger Dam Franciscs, scale measured primarily the interpersonal aspect. Participants were also rated by their peers and junior leaders on the weisings items. Leadership was assessed using a peer nomination system for task-goal and socio-emotional orientation. Both measures but especially the schette et.al. scale, correlated with social desirability, suggesting problems of discriminate validity. Scores on the schutte et.al. scale did not correlate with any peer nominations, indicating questionable convergent validity. In contrast, scores on the weisinger scale (self-report) correlated with peer nominations of socio-emotional leadership and task-goal leadership.

Ciarrochi et.al. (2001) in their study found, despite a great deal of popular interest and the development of numerous training programs in emotional intelligence (EI), some researchers have argued that there is little evidence that EI is both useful and different from other, well established constructs. They hypothesized that E.I. would make a unique contribution to understand the relationship between stress and three important mental health variables, depression, hopelessness and suicidal ideation. University students (m=302) participated in a cross-sectional study that involved measuring like stress, objective and self-reported emotional intelligence and mental health. Regression analysis revealed that stress was associated with greater reported depression, hopelessness and suicidal ideation among people high in emotional perception (EP) compared to others; and greater suicidal ideation among those low in managing other's emotions (MOE). Both EP and MOE were shown to be statistically different from other relevant measures suggesting that EI is a distinctive construct as well as being important in understanding the link between stress and mental health.

Petrides et.al. (2000) in their study examines the role of trait emotional intelligence in academic performance deviant behavior at school on a sample of 650 pupils in British Secondary Education. Trait E.I. moderated the relationship between cognitive ability and academic performance.

Pupils with high trait E.I. scores were less likely to have been excluded from school. Most trait E.I. effects persisted even after controlling for personality variance. It is concluded that the constellation of emotion related self-perceived abilities and dispositions that the construct of trait EI encompasses is implicated in academic performance and deviant behavior, with effects that are particularly relevant to vulnerable or disadvantaged adolescents.

Chan (2003) in his study two hundred and fifty-nine gifted adolescents were assessed on their emotional intelligence and social coping strategies. An item factor analysis yielded four dimensions of emotional intelligence, leading to the construction of 4 empirical scales of emotional intelligence. Students scored most highly on social skills and self-management of emotions, followed by empathy and utilization of emotions. In coping with their being gifted, students endorsed to different degreed their use of 6 coping strategies, which were valuing peer Acceptance, Involvement in Activities, Attempting Avoidance, denying Giftedness, Prizing Conformity and Discounting Popularity. Social skills emerged as the most important components of emotional intelligence predicting the use of strategies of valuing per Acceptance Involvement in Activities.

Brackett, et.al. (2003) in their study assessed the discriminant, criterion and incremental validity of an ability measures of emotional intelligence (EI). College students (N=330) took an ability test of EI, measure of the Big Five personality traits and provided information on life space scale that assessed an array of self-care behaviours, leisure pursuits, academic activities and interpersonal relations. Women scored significantly higher in EI than men. EI, however, was more predictive of the life space criteria for men than for women. Lower EI in males, principally the inability to perceive emotions and to use emotion to facilitate though, was associated with negative outcomes, including illegal drug and alcohol use, deviant behavior and poor relations with friends. The findings remained significant even after statistically controlling for scores on the Big Five and academic achievements. In this sample, EI was significantly associated with maladjustment and negative behaviours for college-aged males but not for females.

Riley, et.al. (2003) in their study explored the relationship between low emotional intelligence and substance use problems in adults. One hundred and forty-one participants completed the Self-Administered Alcoholism Screening Test, the Drug Abuse Screening Test, an Emotional Intelligence

Scale and a measure of psychosocial coping. Low emotional intelligence was a significant predictor of both alcohol-related and drug-related problems. Coping was not found to be a significant mediator between emotional intelligence and substance use problems.

Shanwal (2003) conducted study of correlates and Nurturance of Emotional Intelligence in primary school children, this study points towards a possibility of two factors of Emotional Intelligence. The first factor components show correlation with socio-cultural and environmental variables. The second factor components show association with variables indirectly representing general intelligence like academic achievement. Among the different eco-cultural groups, rural children have higher Emotional Intelligence and rural boys have highest intelligence score, while urban boys are poorest among all the children. Girls have higher Emotional Intelligence in comparisons to boys, rural girls are better at understanding and regulating emotion while urban girls are best at identification of emotion. Better regulators of emotion were also good at academic. Emotional Intelligence shows any relationship with social performance or deftness and alternative abilities. The study delineates that nurturing emotional intelligence have definite positive influence on the overall emotional intelligence of the child. The positive influence of nurturance is not only component specific but also shows spillover effect on the other emotional intelligence factor.

Dash, et.al. (2004) studied 'Teachers' Effectiveness in relation to their Emotional Intelligence', the study attempts to examine the effect of emotional intelligence on teacher's effectiveness at senior secondary level of education. The study was conducted on senior secondary school teachers. From the analysis of the result, it was found that there is a positive effect of emotional intelligence on teacher's effectiveness (as overall and in the entire dimension) at the senior secondary school level. The teacher's effectiveness of various dimensions on differential between high and low emotional intelligence is also found positive.

Mahasundaran et.al. (2004) on a study revealed that there has a significant positive correlation between Emotional Intelligence and academic achievement of teacher trainees at primary level. But the correlation is low. This is because, in Indian situation, the teacher trainees are not aware of knowledge about Emotional Intelligence. They were not trained properly towards Emotional management. So, by providing proper training through curricular and co-curricular activities in Emotional

Intelligence, it could be possible to improve the academic achievement of teacher trainees.

Parker, et.al. (2004), in their study, 'Academic Achievement and Emotional Intelligence: predicting the successful Transitional High School to university', this study examined the impact of Emotional Intelligence on the successful transition from high school to university. The short form of the Emotional Quotient Inventory was completed by 1,426 first year students attending four different universities within the first week of classes. At the end of the academic year the students' cumulative GPA was used to identify two groups of students: academically successful and unsuccessful students' results revealed different emotional and social competencies. These findings suggest that emotional intelligence plays an important role in the successful transition from high school to university.

Nicholas (2005) on a title Adolescents Emotional intelligence in relation to demographic characteristics indicated that Emotional Intelligence Levels were positively related to females, parents' education and household income. Emotional Intelligence scores were significantly different between females and males with females reporting higher emotional intelligence levels.

Zeidner, et.al. (2005) in their study 'Assessing emotional intelligence in gifted and non-gifted high school students: outcomes depend on the measure', this study examined academically gifted (N=83) and non-gifted (N=125) high school students from Israel to compare mean emotional intelligence (EI) scores, various assessment procedures, and relations between EI and ability, across different populations. Participants completed the Mayer-Salovey-Caruso Emotional Intelligence. Test (MSCEIT), the Schutte Self-Report Inventory (SSRI), and the vocabulary subtest of the Hebrew version of the Wechsler intelligence scale for children-revised (WISC-R-19). Gifted students scored higher on the MSCEIT, but lower on the SSRI. Findings suggest that individual differences are measures dependent, with the profile of scores variables across EI assessment procedures. Concepts assessed by the MSCEIT resemble a type of intelligence, whereas findings with the SSRI are problematic from this perspective.

Singaravelu (2006) studied 'Emotional Intelligence of Student Teachers (pre-service) at primary levels in Pondicherry Region.' In this study Emotional Intelligence of student teachers in Pondicherry region was above average as the mean and standard deviation were found to be 33-34 and

9.46 respectively. No significant difference was observed in emotional intelligence between men and women student teachers. Differences were observed in Emotional Intelligence between the groups regarding locality of the residence of student teachers. Hence, locality of residence has a significant effect on emotional intelligence of student teachers. Significant difference was observed in emotional intelligence between the groups regarding material status. Hence, marital status has a significant effect on emotional intelligence of student teachers.

Kaur, et.al. (2006), in their study, teacher's effort to promote Emotional Intelligence among adolescent student found the major finding of the study are in the expected direction and in favour of the hypothesis. The analysis of the total effort shows that the effort which teachers are doing is below average. The teachers are doing the effort maximum on the competency of inter-personal realm and very few on intra-personal realms. And gain this percentage is also far below the average.

Killgore, et.al. (2007), in their study, 'Neural correlates of emotional intelligence in adolescent children,' found the somatic marker hypothesis posits a key role for the ventromedial prefrontal cortex, amygdale and insular in the ability to utilize emotions to guide decision making and behavior. However, the relationship between activity in these brain regions and emotional intelligence (EI) during adolescent, a time of particular importance for emotional and social development have not been studied, sing functional magnetic resonance imaging(FMRI), correlated scores from the bar-on Emotional Quotient Inventory, Youth version with brain activity during perception of fearful faces in 16 healthy children and adolescent. Consistent with the neural efficiency hypothesis, higher EQ correlated negatively with activity in the somatic marker circuitry and other par limbic regions. Positive correlations were observed between EQ and activity in the cerebellum and visual association cortex. The findings suggest that the construct of self-reported EQ in adolescent is inversely related to the efficiency of neural processing within somatic marker circuitry during emotional provocation.

Kaur, et.al. (2007), in their 'strategic emotional intelligence of Punjabi adolescents,' the study was conducted on 200 female adolescents (17-18years) studying in school, Ludhiana city, the socio-economic – status (ses) of the respondents was assessed by administering a standardized socio-economic –scale to assess strategic emotional intelligence. Results revealed that majority (86%) of the respondents exhibited high performance level for understanding emotion and remaining were almost equally distribute over the next two levels i.e. competent and consider developing for managing emotions distribution or respondents over the three levels was equally distributed. Similar distribution was observed for strategic emotional intelligence. Further high performance for understanding emotions does not guarantee high performance for managing emotions for both understanding and managing emotions make an individual high performer for strategic emotional intelligence.

Stell, et.al. (2007), in their study under 'Trait Emotional Intelligence, psychological well-being and peer-rated social competence in adolescence', where they found, the trait emotion intelligence framework provides comprehensive coverage of emotion-related self-perceptions and dispositions. In this study, we investigated the relationship between trait EI and four distinct socio-emotional criteria on a sample of Dutch adolescents (N=282, 136 girls, 146 boys; mean age =13.75years). As hypothesized, trait EI was positively associated with adaptive coping styles and negatively associated with depressive thoughts and frequency of somatic complaints. It was also negatively associated with depressive thoughts and frequency of somatic complaints. It was also negatively associated with maladaptive coping styles in boys only. Adolescents with high trait EI scores received more nominations from their classmates for being co-operative and girls gave significantly more nominations to classmates with high trait EI scores for having leadership qualities. The discussion focuses on the operationalization of trait emotional self-efficacy in adolescents.

Joseph, et.al. (2007), in their study, 'measuring emotional intelligence in adolescent', study conducted among one-hundred and thirty-one students (aged 13-15) completed a self-report measure of emotional intelligence (SEI) and a number of other, theoretically relevant measures. They were then induced into either a positive, negative or neutral mood and asked to complete a task that assessed mood management behavior. We found that EI was reliably measured in adolescents was higher for females than males and was positively associated with skill at identifying emotional expressions, amount of social support, extent of satisfaction with social support and mood management behavior. These relationships help even after controlling for two constructs that potentially overlap with EI, namely self-esteem and trait anxiety. The study offers evidence that the SEI is a distinctive and useful measure.

Downney, et.al. (2008), in their study, 'Emotional Intelligence and Scholastic achievement in Australian adolescents', examined the relationship between emotional intelligence (EI) and scholastic achievement in Australian adolescents. Two hundred and nine secondary school students (86 males and 123 females) each completed the Adolescent Swinburne University Emotional Intelligence Test (SUEIT) and academic achievement data was collected for all subjects from year seven to eleven. Academic success was found to be associated with higher levels of total EI, via assessment of the EI of different academic level (80th percentile, 20th percentile and middle groups). Regressions analysis also revealed that dimensions of the adolescent SUEIT differentially predicated secondary school subject grades: Emotional management and control was found to significantly predict Maths (r2 =0.06) and Science (r2 =0.04); the understanding Emotions sub-scale significantly predicted scores for Art (r2 =0.12) and Geography (r2 =0.08). It was conducted that the development of EI may after educator's significant opportunities to improve scholastic performance and emotional competencies.

Shah, et.al. (2008), in their study under, 'perceived Emotional Intelligence and ways of coping among students, in this study the sample comprised of 197 students between the age of 18 and 25 years. Participants completed self-reported measures of emotional intelligence and ways of coping. It was found that appraisal of emotions in the self was positively correlated with plan full problem solving and positive reappraisal coping styles. Appraisal of emotions in others was positive reappraisal. Emotional regulation of the self was positively correlated with plan full problem solving, confronting coping, self-controlling, positive reappraisal and with distancing but negatively correlated with escape avoidance. No gender differences were found in perceived emotional intelligence and ways of coping except for self-control where males reported higher than females.

Mangal (2009). Emotional Intelligence Inventory for the measurement of student emotional intelligence in respect of four areas, namely, Intra-personal Awareness (knowing about one's own emotions), Inter-personal awareness (knowing about other's emotions), Intra-personal management (managing one's own emotion) and Inter-personal management(managing one's own emotion) and inter-personal management) respectively.

Singh, et.al. (2009), Emotional Intelligence and medium of instruction: a study among secondary school teachers, they found a teacher who has a strong emotional bondage with students. In recent time, there is a race towards English medium School among parents. Parents have a feeling that their wards can get better education as well as better opportunity for their overall developments in English Medium School. Research has been carried out on 140 teachers (70 each from Hindi medium And English Medium Schools), the research indicates that Emotional Intelligence of secondary school teacher differs significantly in relation to their medium of instruction.

Kelly & Kenneth, (2010) on a title The Differential effects of General Mental Ability and Emotional Intelligence on Academic performance and social interaction discussed whether Emotional Intelligence has incremental validity over and above traditional intelligence dimensions. It is proposed that Emotional Intelligence and general mental ability differ in predicting academic performances and the quality of social interaction among college students. Using student's samples from two different colleges, it was found that Emotional Intelligence and General Mental Ability each have unique power to predict academic performances and that General mental Ability is the stronger predictor.

Antonius (2010) on a title Social Intelligence and Academic achievement as predictors of Adolescent popularity where the participants were 512, 14-15 yrs old adolescents (56% boys, 44% girls) in vocational and college preparatory schools in North-Western Europe. Study found that perceived popularity was significantly related to social intelligence, but not academic achievement in both contexts.

Pettit, Mitchele L, (2010) assessed relationship between perceived Emotional Intelligence factors and eating disorder symptoms among male and female college students. Results confirmed gender differences regarding eating disorder symptoms and indicated that low level of perceived Emotional Intelligence are associated with greater risk of bulimia/food preoccupation.

From the above reviews, it was observed that emotional intelligence is the driving force for affecting both personal and social interaction. Interaction process is a much appreciated communication process to help people know each other with hearty, cordial harmony. It is proved by the research that Emotional Intelligence is very important factors not only to achieve academic excellence but also to achieve success an all sphere of life. These prompted the investigator to put forth a strong rationale for the study.

CHAPTER THREE

METHODOLOGY

3.1 RESEARCH DESIGN

A normative survey was adopted to find the relationship between emotional Intelligence of senior secondary school students with respect to their age and gender. A descriptive study design was considered to be appropriate method of investigation for the study. Other method of study such as the historical and the experimental methods of study were not considered to be suitable because of the nature of the objective of the study .In a historical method, phenomenon, event or condition is analyzed by the investigator with regards to the factor operating in the past. An experimental method of study was also not deemed fit for the present study as not control situation was adopted. Therefore the study was primarily a descriptive study design of ex-post facto type.

3.2 POPULATION OF THE STUDY

Out of 15 senior secondary schools, 5 schools were selected on simple random basis. Out of 1000 students present in classes XI and XII of these 5 senior secondary schools, 100 students were selected on simple random basis.

3.3 SAMPLE OF THE STUDY

The Sample of the study consists of 5 Senior Secondary Schools of Darjeeling District. The samples were 100 students out of which 25 girls and 25 boys from class XI and 25 girls and 25 boys from class XII. Age of the class XI students is of 17 years and age of class XII students 18 years.

The table presented below gives the descriptive sample characteristics.

Table 1: Descriptive sample characteristics

Variation	Sub Sample	Total no. of studs selected	No. of studs participated for the study
Class XI	BOYS	25	25
	GIRLS	25	25
Class XII	BOYS	25	25
	GIRLS	25	25
Age	Boys(17yrs)	25	25
	Girls(17yrs	25	25
	Boys(18yrs)	25	25
	Girls(18yrs)	25	25
Total	Boys		50
	Girls		50

25 Boys and 25 Girls of class XI aged 17 years and 25 boys and 25 girls of class XII aged 18 years were selected for the administration of the Emotional Intelligence scale.

3.4 TOOLS USED

Emotional Intelligence Inventory of Mangal and Mangal (2009) is used as the meaning instrument for the study. A brief description along with technical features is given below.

The Emotional Intelligence Inventory (EII)

Emotional Intelligence Inventory has been designed for use with Hindi and English knowing 16+years of school, college and university students for the measurement of their emotional intelligence (total as well as separately) in respect of four areas or aspect of emotional intelligence namely, Intra-personal Awareness (knowing about one own emotion), Inter-personal Awareness (knowing about other emotion), Intra-personal Management (Managing one's own emotions) and Inter-personal Management (Managing others emotions) respectively.

Table 2: Areas or Aspect of Emotional Intelligence Inventory

Sl. No	Area/Aspect	No.of Items
(a)	Intra-Personal Awareness(Own emotions)	25
(b)		25
	Inter-Personal Awareness(Others emotions)	
(c)		25
(d)	Intra-Personal Management(Own emotions)	25
	Inter-Personal Management(Other emotions)	
	Total Items	100

It has 100 items, 25 each from the four areas to be answered as yes or no,indicating complete agreement or disagreement with the proposed statement respectively .For scoring one mark in to provided for the response indicating presence of emotional intelligence and zero for the absence of emotional intelligence . Table 3 shows the scoring scheme of Emotional Intelligence Inventory.

Table 3: Scoring Scheme of Emotional Intelligence Inventory

	Mode of Response	Score
S.No of Items (Where 'yes' response shows presence of Intelligence). 6,18,19,20,29 to25,27 to 29,31,41,to 44,51 to 56,58 to 68,70,71,73to 76,79 to 82,84,88 to 90,96,99	Yes / No	01 / 0
S.No.of Items(Where "No" response shows presence of Intelligence) 1to5,7to17,21,22,26,30,32to40,45to50,57,69,72,77,78,85 to,87,91to95,97,98,100	No / Yes	01 / 0

3.5 TECHNIQUES FOR DATA ANALYSIS

To collect data from the selected sample, the questionnaire techniques were adopted. Their responses to the questions were recorded by the subjects on an answer sheet provided with the test booklet, and scoring was done according to the manual prescribed .For assessment Descriptive Statistics were used. Inferential Statistics for differentiating the contrast like 't' ratio were used to the intra-variable in all components and also for total emotional intelligence.

3.6 PROCEDURE

A two assessment design (i.e. for XI and XII students) to collect Emotional Intelligence and its relationship towards gender and age is administered to the student in an introductory or homeroom type class to ensure a more wide speed sampling of students. Consent is obtained from individual prior to participation.

For collecting data pertaining to Emotional Intelligence, the reusable test booklet as well as separate answer sheet were distributed to each student. After all of the information which is collected ,a total score is completed for each students.

CHAPTER FOUR

ANALYSIS AND INTERPRETATION

4.1 ADMINISTRATION OF THE TEST & COLLECTION OF DATA.

First of all, the head of the institutions of all 5 Senior Secondary Schools were contacted by the Investigation and permission was sought from them to reach the corresponding class for the purpose of test administration and data collection. The investigation did it well in advance and tried the dates and timing for the same purpose.

Firstly the investigator establishes report between the students and expressed the purpose for coming to their class. They were told to be as free as possible because nothing to be worried about the response would be very confidential and would be used for research purposely. An information sheet was handed one to each pupil in order to record their personal data, class, sex, age etc.

A suitable time was fixed and the investigator administered the "Emotional Intelligence Scale" over the sample of the students i.e. 25 boys & 25 girls from class XI and 25 boys and 25 girls from class XII, total 100 students, who were selected and who were very much willing to participate in the study.

4.2. COLLECTION OF DATA THROUGH ADMINISTRATION OF THE SCALE

The investigator administered the emotional intelligence scale as group test the administration procedure for the tools was followed as per norms and conditions laid down by Ebel and Frisbie(1991).

Following precaution was observed during administration.

- The instruction for administration the scale was read at first and every bit was explained to the sample under investigation.

- During test administration, the investigation ensured proper sitting arrangement for the sample and read the instruction slowly, clearly and loudly so that the students understood the mood of responding to the scale.
- The investigation took care to see that each student followed the correct working procedure in the answer sheet.
- No time limit was required to complete the test.
- The testers were asked to clarify their doubt initially.
- No two tests were simultaneously administered on the same group of subjects in the same day.
- All the subjects were provided with pencils and answer-sheets for responding to the items of the test.

4.3. SCORING THE SCALE

All the scales were score as per scoring manual given by Mangal & Mangal Emotional Intelligence Inventory (2009). The answer sheet were collected, hand scored and the total number of correct answer was counted to arrived at the total raw score of the respondent along with the total score of each component area.

The data thus collected were tabulated both component wise and total emotional intelligence score wise which served the basis for interpretation of result in accordance with the objective and hypothesis formulated.

4.4 DISTRIBUTION OF SCORES ON EMOTIONAL INTELLIGENCE

After collection of data exploratory method such as frequency tables and descriptive statistics were used to have a feel for the data.

Distribution of score on the Emotional Intelligence Scale

Table 4: Frequency Distribution on EIS=100

Class Intervals	Frequency	Boys	Girls	C.F Total	C.F %	Smooth Frequency	C.F% Boys	C.F% Girls
75-80	03	02	01	100	100	6	100	100
70-75	15	10	05	97	97	13	96	98
65-70	21	09	12	82	82	20.33	76	88
55-65	25	11	14	61	61	21	58	64
55-60	17	10	07	36	36	17.33	36	36
50-55	10	03	07	19	19	11.66	16	22
45-50	08	05	03	09	09	6.33	10	8
40-45	01	00	01	01	01	3	-	2
Total	100	50	50					

On perusal of the above table, it was revealed that the modal class interval is (60-65) and there have been gradual tapering of frequencies both towards the upper and lower ends. The same is also in the case of sub samples of boys and girls.

Distribution of scores needs to be presented in histogram and frequency polygon with smooth frequency polygon super imposed on it in order to study normality in distribution.

From the nature of the frequency distribution as it has already been observed that maximum scores been clustered at the modal class interval in all the cases it gives a primary outlook of normal distribution. Therefore it was felt obligatory to calculate the descriptive measure of samples and sub-samples.

The graphical representation of the scores on Emotional Intelligence along with frequency polygon are presented separately in three figures for the total samples and to two sub samples of boys and girls in figure(i), figure(ii) and figure(iii) respectively.

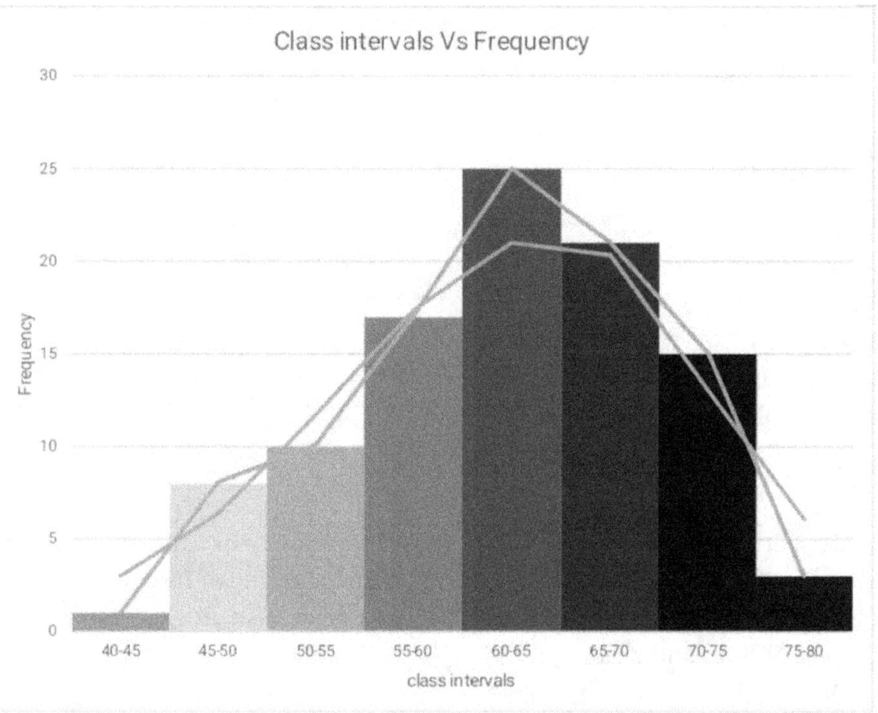

Figure (i). Histogram and Frequency polygon with smooth Frequency polygon

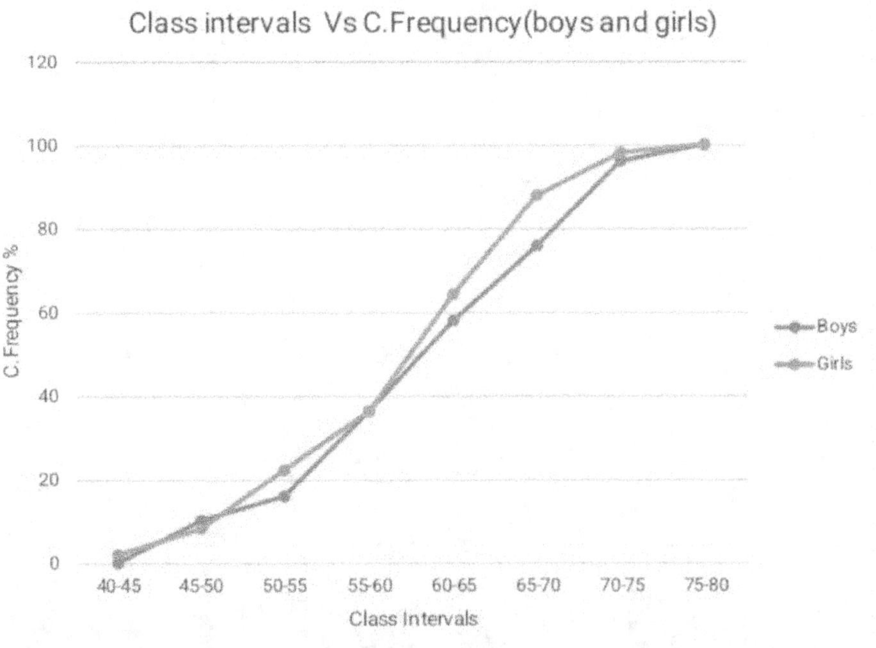

Figure (ii).Ogive for total sample and two sub-sample of boys and girls

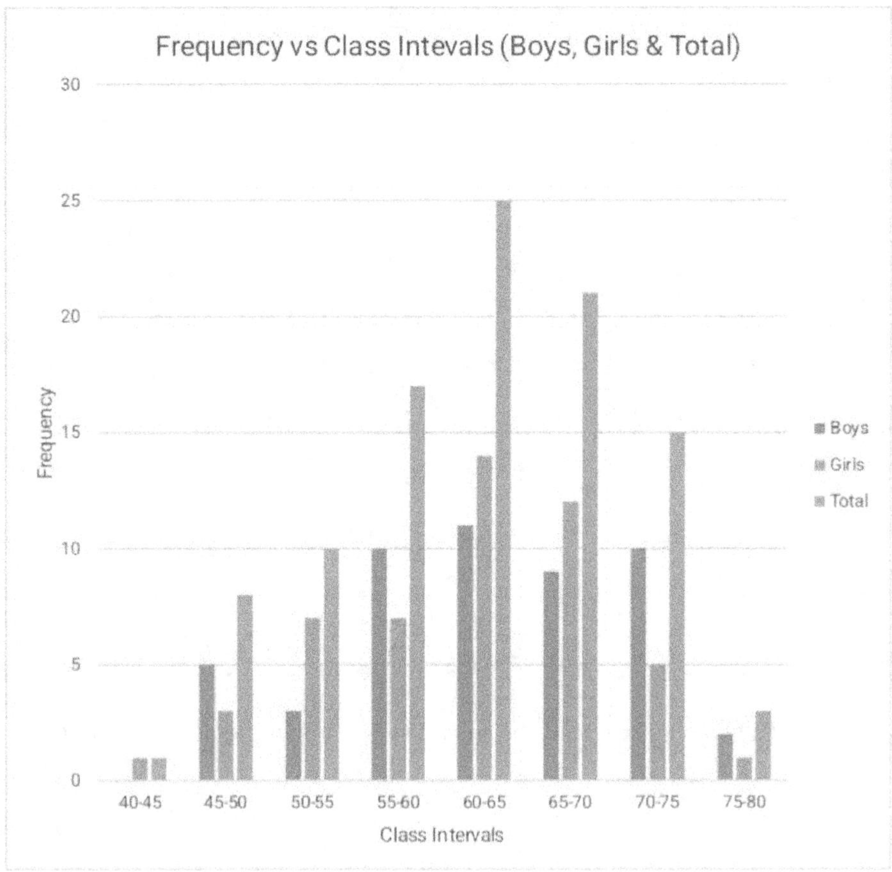

Figure (iii).Multiple Bar-Diagram representing scores of Boys, Girls and Total Samples

4.5 DESCRIPTIVE MEASURE ON EMOTIONAL INTELLIGENCE

Means and standard deviation of all the components of the score and the total score were calculated as a part of descriptive statistics and for verification of hypothesis inferential statistics was applied. In order to test the distribution of scores along the lines of normality, the measures of central tendency, variation, quartile, deviation, percentile score, skewness and kurtosis have been computed and presented in table 5.

Table 5: Central tendency, SD, Quartile deviation, Percentile, and Skewness and Kurtosis

	N	M	Mdn	Mo	SD	Q1	Q3	P10	P90	Skewness	Kurtosis	Q
Total	100	62.1	62.8	64.2	7.64	56.76	68.33	50.5	72.6	-0.2	0.25	5.7

The descriptive measure on Emotional Intelligence Score revealed that the sample mean, median, mode was found to be 62.1, 62.8 and 64.2 respectively. The semi-inter quartile range(Q)being 5.78 when added to the median gives a value of 68.58 and when Q was subtracted from the median the value is 57.02 which reveal that they are not the same. Therefore the distribution could not be confirmed to be normal.

Then in order to test the distribution along the lines of normality skewness and kurtosis were calculated by applying appropriate formulae. It was revealed that the skewness of the curve found to be -0.27 and kurtosis was found to 0.25 as against 0 and 0.263 respectively. These values clearly reveal that the distribution of scores on Emotional Intelligence Score was negatively skewed and Platykurtic.

The scores were then calculated as per the conditions of normality in respect of inclusion of percentages of cases within +- 16 limits,+-26 limits and +-36 limits. In order to categories the adolescent in different levels of Emotional Intelligence. These limits were considered for this the number of sample was categorized under five heads and their score ranges were calculated along with the number of persons contained in those limits. The same has been presented in table 6.

Table 6: Category in accordance with the level of Emotional Intelligence

Categories	Limits of Raw Score	Percentage
High	78 & above	0
Above average	70-77	18
Average	50-70	63
Below average	45-55	18
Poor	44 & below	01

On perusal of above the above table it was revealed that the score on Emotional Intelligence have not been obtained in the right direction might have been due to the fact that the sample is very small and the assumed that the skewness of the curve being -0.27 it approached almost normality. In view of the above the the investigator desires to conclude that the result obtained in the study may be treated as appropriate and a normal.

4.6 Descriptive measures on the total emotional intelligence scale in relation to the intra-variable of gender, age and component wise.

After frequency distribution the scores were tabulated as per the intra-variables of gender, age and component wise were calculated. The result has been presented in table 7.

Table 7: Mean and SD of the total sample on total emotional Intelligence in relation to all the intra-variables:

Variations	Sub-Sample	Number N	Mean M	Standard Deviation
Gender	Boys	50	62.4	4.49
	Girls	50	61.6	4.72
Age	17 yrs	50	57.5	2.76
	18 yrs	50	66.5	5.45
Total		100	62.1	7.64

On perusal of the above table it was evident the Emotional Intelligence mean score in case of gender differences is minimum whereas in case of age differences it has sizeable differences in the mean score. While comparing the mean score of Boys and girls with total mean score it was found that mean score of boys exceed total mean score while mean score of girls is lower than total mean score, like wise in age group in 18 yrs, it exceed total mean score while for the age group o 17 yrs it lies far below the total mean scores.

Further the mean and standard deviation on Emotional Intelligence scales were calculated component wise and sub sample wise. The result was presented in table 8.

Table 8: Component wise mean and SD of Boys and Girls

Variations	Sub samples	N	Mean	SD
	Girls	50	14.6	2.7
Intra personal awareness	Boys	50	16.3	2.4
Inter personal awareness	Boys	50	16.1	3
	Girls	50	15.3	3.1
Intra personal Management	Boys	50	16.3	3.6
	Girls	50	16.8	3.3
Inter personal Management	Boys	50	16.6	3.05
	Girls	50	16.5	4.7

On perusal of above table it was revealed that the mean scores in case of Intra personal and Inter personal awareness, the mean scores of boys are greater than mean scores of girls showing thereby superiority of the boys over girls.

In case of Inter personal management girls exceed the mean score of boys but in their personal management boys are superior to girls. A comparative picture of these mean scores sub sample wise and component wise has been presented in fig (iv).

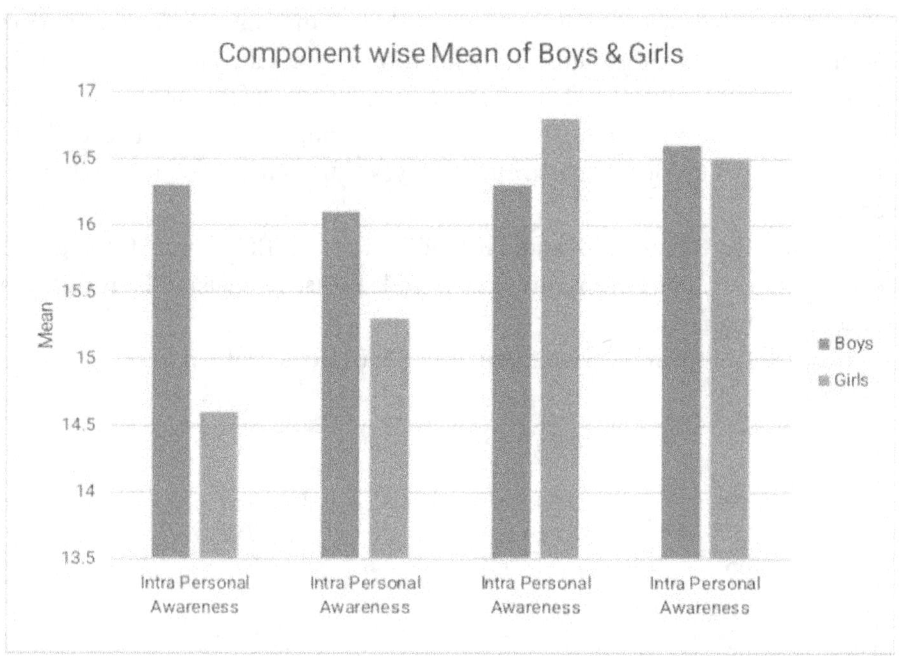

Figure (iv).Component wise Bar- Diagram

Table 9: Mean, SD and 't' test result for differences between mean Emotional Intelligence scores of boys &girls.

Group	N	M	SD	SED	't'	Remarks
Boys	50	62.4	4.49			
				0.91	0.87	NS
Girls	50	61.6	4.72			

On perusal of the above table, it was concluded that the calculated value of 't' (0.87) is less than the table value of 't' (1.67 at 0.05 and 2.390 at

0.01) level of significance. Therefore null hypothesis formulated earlier that "these doesn't exist significant difference in Emotional Intelligence in relation to gender variation" could not be rejected, that means the alternative hypothesis that the mean scores of boys and girls are equal could be tanable.

From this result the investigator desire to conclude that boys and girls in the sample display equal magnitude of emotional Intelligence.

The result is not in confirmative with the studied of Ciarrochi et.al.(2007) and Nicolas (2005) where there was significant difference in Emotional Intelligence due to gender variation where girls reporting higher Emotional Intelligence compare to boys. However in the study of Mangal and Mangal (2009) the Emotional Intelligence of male and female students show in terms of percentile scores and it was observed that there was not much difference in intrapersonal &interpersonal management due to gender variation. In view of the above the investigator has adopted the Emotional Intelligence scale of Mangal and Mangal. Non-significant difference in gender variation in the present study was treated as most appropriate.

However when component wise gender difference in Emotional Intelligence was studied a significant difference was obtained in case of interpersonal awareness. This gave ample evidence in support of the hypothesis. The result of component wise summary of 't' ratio has been presented in table 11. The other 't' ratio could not be significant.

Table 10: Component wise mean & SD and 't' test on Emotional Intelligence of adolescents.

Component	N	M	SD	SED	"t"	Remarks
Intra Personal awareness	50	16.3	2.4	0.5	3.4	S
	50	14.6	2.7			
Inter personal awareness	50	16.1	3	0.61	1.31	NS
	50	15.3	3.1			
Intra-Personal Management	50	16.3	3.6	0.68	0.73	NS
	50	16.8	3.3			
Inter-Personal Management	50	16.6	3.05			
	50	16.5	4.7			

't' for dt 98 at 0.05 level 1.980 at 0.01 level 2.617

4.7 AGE DIFFERENCE IN EMOTIONAL INTELLIGENCE.

In order to find out the effect of age in Emotional Intelligence, samples were split into two group i.e. 50 samples of age group of 17 year and another samples of the age group of 18 yrs, 't' ratio was calculated to locate difference if any in the age group for Emotional Intelligence. The result has been presented below.

Table 11: Mean SD & 't' test result for difference between mean emotional intelligence score for different age group

Groups	N	M	S.D	SED	"t"	Remarks
18 yrs	50	66.5	5.45			
17 yrs	50	57.5	2.76	0.93	9.67	S

On perusal of the above table, it was concluded that the calculated value of 't' (9.67) is more than the table value of 't' (1.67 at 0.05 and 2.390 at 0.01) level of significance. Therefore null hypothesis formulated earlier that "there doesn't exist significant difference in Emotional Intelligence in relation to age variation "was rejected ,that means the alternative hypothesis is accepted i.e. the observed difference in the age variance in Emotional Intelligence is marked significant. Age contribute much to intellectual development because maturity counts much in the development of social and emotional intelligence in children. In that context of study of Majoribnks (1971) have given evidence that mental maturity of 11 years old boys are inferior to 16 years boys. This indicates the age difference in level of intelligence. In this direction the study Salovey and Mayer(1990) found that EQ developed with increasing age and experience as a person progress from childhood to adulthood.

CHAPTER FIVE

SUMMARY AND CONCLUSION

According to the modern psychologist, the emotional intelligence is responsible for the success of a person. For every man's success intelligence quotient contribute about 2o% to the factors that determine success in life.

The remaining 80% contributed by emotional intelligence. Goleman (1995) has defined emotional intelligence as the capacity for recognizing our own feelings and those of others, for motivating ourselves and in our relationships. It describe ability distinct form, but complementary to academics intelligence. According to Goleman,a key set of characteristics makes up emotional intelligence are self awareness, self regulation, motivation, Empathy and social skills. In order to survive in a fast changing and competitive world, every person needs to develop and nurture emotional intelligence.

Therefore the concept of emotional intelligence leads to a more magnified study of its factors which arises a need for reviews to arrive at the problem of the study.

RATIONALE OF THE STUDY

From the reviews of researches it is quite clear that Emotional Intelligence is the driving force behind the factors that affect personal success and everyday interaction with others. Studies of Emotional Intelligence have shown its relevance to many aspects of life and the role it plays in the interaction and discussion of any given day. However ,as almost all Emotional Intelligence research targets adults, a need exists for the exploration of adolescent's Emotional Intelligence as adolescent need to develop empathy ,self awareness, self regulations and social skills in order to grow socially and emotionally for a better world of prosperity. Hence these have been a need in assessing the emotional intelligence of adolescent and provide necessary guidance to see better world.

OBJECTIVES OF THE STUDY

For this study, the following objectives have been framed:

* To assess the Emotional Intelligence of senior secondary school students with respect to their age and gender.
* To compare the levels of emotional intelligence of senior secondary school students in relation to intra & inter-personal awareness and intra & inter-personal management.
* To categorize them under differential levels of emotional intelligence along the lines of normality in a five point scale.
* To find differential levels of emotional intelligence due to age and gender variations.

FORMULATION OF HYPOTHESIS

The following hypotheses have been formulated in null form keeping in view the objectives of the study:

Ho1: Emotional Intelligence in senior secondary school students is not normally displayed.

Ho2: There doesn't exist significant difference in intrapersonal awareness of senior secondary school students due to gender variation.

H03: There doesn't exist significant difference in interpersonal awareness of senior secondary school students due to gender variation.

Ho4: There doesn't exist significant difference in intrapersonal management of senior secondary school students due to gender variation.

Ho5: There doesn't exist significant difference in interpersonal management of senior secondary school students due to gender variation.

Ho6: There doesn't exist significant difference in Emotional Intelligence of senior secondary school students due to age variation.

H07: There doesn't exist significant difference in Emotional Intelligence of senior secondary school students due to gender variation.

OPERATIONAL DEFINITION

Emotional Intelligence: In this study, emotional intelligence refer to inter and intra personal awareness and management as per Mangal and Mangal(2009).

Senior School students include students between the age group of 17-18 yrs and reading in classes XI-XII in Senior Secondary schools.

SCOPE AND DELIMITATION

Due to stringency of time and money in collecting data only 100 students of class XI and XII from 5 Sr. Secondary Schools were considered for the study. The scope of this study was limited to the extent of assessing Emotional Intelligence of senior School Students with respect to their gender and age. The study is delimited to students of XI and class XII of 5 Senior Secondary Schools only.

METHODOLOGY OF STUDY

RESEARCH DESIGN:

In the present investigation normative survey method was employed to find the relationship between emotional intelligence of Senior secondary school with respect to their age and gender.

SAMPLE

Samples were collected from 100 students of which 25 girls and 25 boys from class XI and 25 girls and 25 boys from class XII from 5 Sr . Sec . schools.

TOOLS USED

Emotional Intelligence Inventory of Mangal and Mangal (2009) for measuring Emotional intelligence of adolescents was used.

TECHNIQUES FOR DATA ANALYSIS

Various statistical techniques was used in the analysis of the data .The data obtained will be subjected to different statistical techniques.

i.Questionnaire technique for administration and scoring .

ii.Descriptive statistics for assessment .

iii.Inferential statistics for differentiating the contrasts like 't' ratio and sinteraction analysis.

PROCEDURE

A two part assessment design (i.e., for XI and XII students) to collect Emotional Intelligence in relation to the variations of gender and age was administered to the students in an or homeroom type class to ensure a more wide speed sampling of students. Consents were obtained from all individuals prior to participation. After all of the information which is collected, a total score was competed for each student.

MAJOR FINDINGS

Results obtained were discussed in the light of the objectives and hypothesis framed. The null hypotheses tested for significance in the results section have been interpreted in terms of rejection and acceptance depending upon the result.

*Emotional Intelligence Adolescent is not normally distributed , however the skewness of the curve being- 0.27 it approached almost normality .Therefore the result obtained in the study may be treated as appropriate and normal.

*Gender wise different in emotion intelligence Null hypothesis formulated earlier that these does not exist significant difference in emotion intelligence in relation to gender variance could not be rejected .However the result is not in confirmative with the studies of Clarrochi et . al. (2007) and Nicholas (2005) where these were significant different in emotional intelligence due to gender variations.

*Component wise difference in emotional intelligence was studied a significant difference in case of inter-personal awareness. This gave ample evidence in support of the hypothesis. However for other component 't' ration could not be significant.

*Age wise difference in emotional intelligence Null hypothesis formulated earlier that there does not exist significant difference in emotional intelligence in relation to age variance could be rejected. In that contact of studies Majoribnks(1971,1972) have given evidences that mental maturity of 11 years old boys are inferior to 16 years boys.

CONCLUSION

It is concluded that there does not exist significant difference in Emotional Intelligence of higher school students due to gender variation but there is significant difference in emotional intelligence of higher school students.

FURTHER IMPLICATION OF THE STUDY

*A similar study may be conducted to validate the present findings.

* A similar study may be conducted on a larger sample taking all the schools of Sikkim.

* A similar study can be conducted by taking into consideration of other variables.

* A comparative study of relationship between age and sex in assessing emotional intelligence can be undertaken among students of different states and different countries.

* The study also gives indications in which aspects either boys or the girls are inferior.

Necessary careers guidance and counseling can be given during this period for developing that aspect of emotional intelligence in them.

* In the school, colleges and / or universities the teacher play role to improve EQ among the students by providing adequate environmental activity based example and illustrations in the class. The Teacher should acknowledge accept and emphases with the feeling of their students. They should create the salubrious environment for the students in a positive way and direct them to think of all possible solutions of their own way. In work place and elsewhere with the improvement of interpersonal relationship among students and/Or persons who are related to that works or situations and / or persons who are related, To that work or situation IQ can be nurtured by them. In adolescent stage to avoid loneliness, Lacks of concentration, being stubborn, drug abuse, feeling unsolved and many more problems emotional intelligence concept should be introduced in all level of education system.

Bibliography

Antonius, H.N. (2010). Social intelligence and Academics achievement As predictors of Adolescent popularity ,Journal of Youth and Adolescent V.39 P:62-72.

Bachman (2000). The influence of Emotional intelligence on the Collectors of collection agency. Retrieved june 26, 2003 from http://www.ei.consortium.org. In Cary Cherniss (Ed) . The Business care for Emotional intelligence.

Brackett,M.A.et.al.(2003). Emotional intelligence and its relation To everyday behavior, university of New Hamshrine, Department of Psychology, Durham; available on http://www.goggle.com.

Chan,D.W.(2003). Dimensions of emotional intelligence and their Relationship with social coping among Gifted Adolescent in Hongkong, Journal of youth Adolescence, springer Netherland available on http://www.goggle.com.

Charbonneau, D. (2001). Emotional intelligence & leadership in Adolescent, Department of military psychology and leadership, Canada 17,available on http://www.goggle.com.

Ciarrochi, J. et.al. (2001). Emotional intelligence Moderates the relation between stress and mental health, Department of psychology, University of Wollongong 2522, available http/www.googlecom.

Coover. Et.al. (200). A study of Relationship between self identity and Academic persistence and Achievement Ma countersterotypical domain, available on htpp://www.google.com.

Dash, D.N. et.al. (2004). Teacher Effectiveness in Relation to their Emotional Intelligence, Journal of Indian Education, Vol. XXX No 3

Downey, L.A. et. al. (2008). Emotional Intelligence and Scholastic achievement in Australian adolescent, Australian journal of Psychology, Vol. 60, Brain Sciences Institute Swinburne University, Australia.

Ducette et.al.(1984). In S.purphit and S.Nayak's enhancing Personal effectiveness ,training instrument for students, Teachers and Parents, New Delhi-8; Tata MC Graw –hill publishing company.

Ghosh, P.(2003). Emotional Intelligence. everyman's science Vol.xxxviii, No-2.

Gill,V. (2003). Emotional Quotient more important than IQ. The Tribune,13th may,P-13.

Goleman,D. (1995). Emotional Intelligence ,New York : Bantan Books.

Joshep, C, et.al. (2007). Measuring Emotional Intelligence in adolescent, Department of Human Development and sociology, Punjab Agricultural University, Ludhiana, available on htpp://www.goggle.com.

Kaur, S,J. et.al. (2006). Teachers Efforts to promote emotional Intelligence among Adolescent Students, University News, Vol. 44, No. 39.

Kaur, S.J.et. al.(2006). teacher's efforts to promote emotional Intelligence among adolescent students ,University News, vol.44,no.39.

Kelly,Z.(2010). Intelligence,V.38,137-143; Orlando: Elsewhere Publication.

Killgore W. D.,et.al.(2007). 'Neural correlates of emotional Intelligence in adolescent children,'MC Lean Hospital ,Harvard Medicnal Schools, Belmont, Massachusettes, USA, available on http://www.goggle.com.

Kramer (2010). Social and Emotional learning in the kindergarten Classroom; Early childhoods Educational Journal: v.37,P 303-309.

Lefcourt (1976). In S.purphit and S. Nayak's enhancing personal Effectiveness,training instruments for students ,teachers and parents New Delhi-8; Tata MC Graw –Hill publishing company.

Mangal, S.K. et.al. (2009). Emotional Intelligence inventory ,National psychological corporations: Agra,4.

Marjoribaks,K.(1971).Relationship between mental ability and home environment of 11 year and 16 years of old boys, available on htpp://www.google.com.

Mayer (2008). Emotional Intelligence; New Ability or Eclectic traits, American psychologist association V.63 p. 503-517.

Mayer, et.al. (1989). Emotional Intelligence meets traditional Standards for intelligence /27 (4) ,University news ,New Delhi.

Mitchele, L. (2010) .Assessment of perceived emotional intelligence And eating habits among college students: Ameicans Journal of healthEducation: v.41,P.46-52.

Mohan S. K.et.al. (2004). Emotional Intelligence and Achievement of teacher trainees at primary level; journal of Indian Educational review: v.42 No.8.

Nicholas, R.(2005). Adolescent emotional intelligence in relation to Demographic characteristics; san Diego: libra publication.

Parker,J.D.A.et.al. (2006).'Academics achievements and emotional Intelligence: predicting the successful transition from high school to University,'journal of the first year experience and students in transition

Vol.17;University of south California.

Petrides, K.V.et.al.(2002). The role of trait emotional intelligence in Academics performances and deviant behavior of school institute of Education, university of London,25 Woburn square, available http://www.goggle.com.

Reuven, B. (1998). Emotional Intelligence and achievement of Airforce recruiters retrieved June 26,2003 from http:///www.ei.consortium.org. in Cary cherniss (Ed). The business care for emotional intelligence.

Riley,H.et.al.(2003). Low emotional intelligence as predictors of Substance-use problems, university of New England armidale, available on http://www.goggle.com.

Rotter (1954). In S.Punhit & S. Nayak's enhancing personal Effectiveness ,training instruments for students teachers and parents. Tata MC Graw –Hill publishing company Ltd.New Delhi-8.

Salovey and Mayer (1990). what is emotional intelligence? In P. Salovey and D.J.Slytet(Eds) . emotional development and emotional Intelligence. New York; Basic Books.

Salovey, P et.al.(1997). What is emotional intelligence? In P Salovey And D.J.Slytet(Eds) emotional development and emotional intelligence New York; Basic Books.

Seligham (1991). In S.Purohit & S. Nayak's Enhancing personal Effectiveness, training instrument for students,teachers and parents , New-Delhi-8;Tata MC Graw – hill publishing company.

Shah.M.et.al. (2008).'Perceived emotional intelligence and ways of coping Among students', journal of the Indian Academy of Applied psychology, Vol.34;pune.

Shanwal,V.K.(2003). A study of correlates and nurtures of Emotional intelligence in primary school childrens, www.jmi.ac.in/Research/ab 2003 education vinodkumarshanwal.htm.

Singaravelu, S.(2006).'Emotional intelligence of students teachers (pre-service) at primary level of pundicherry regions,' available on http://www.goggle.com.

Singh,G.et.al.(2007). Emotional intelligence and medium of instruction: A study among secondary school teachers, experiments in Education,vol.XXXVII,No.3.

Spencer,L.M.J.R.(1997). Analysis of emotional intelligence of top Level executives . retrieved june 26,2003 from http://www.ei.consortium.org. In cary cherniss(Eds) . the business care for emotional intelligence.

BIBLIOGRAPHY

Stella, M.et.al .(2007). Traits emotional intelligence psychological Well being and peer rated social competence in adolescent,' British journal Of Developmental psychology ,vol.25; British psychological society.

Wechsler,D.(1940). In Kaur ,S.J.& Kaur Harjits's teacher efforts To promote emotional intelligence among adolescent students,university News,vol.44,No.39.

Zeidner,M.et.al.(2005).'Assessing emotional intelligence in gifted And non gifted high school students : outcomes depend on the measure,'University of Haifa ,Isreal; university of Cincinnati,USA ;available online, http://www.goggle .com.